Scalia:
A Brief Look

Caroline Mather Brown

Copyright © 2017 Caroline Mather Brown

Cover image copyright © 2017 3BN Digital

All rights reserved

ISBN: 1542330181

ISBN-13: 978-1542330183

DEDICATION

To the People

CONTENTS

	Acknowledgments	i
1	Prologue	7
2	Can we post the Ten Commandments in the county courthouse?	11
	McCreary County v. ACLU (2005)	
3	Who is "my neighbor"?	19
	D. C. v. Heller (2008)	
4	"One nation"?	29
	Arizona v. U.S. (2012)	
5	What's "unreasonable" searching in the 21st century?	38
	U. S. v. Jones (2012); *Maryland v. King* (2013); *Florida v. Jardines* (2013)	
6	"Cruel" or "unusual" punishment?	47
	Glossip v. Gross (2015)	
7	The outcome overall	57
	Further reading	59
	Index	60
	About the author	64

ACKNOWLEDGMENTS

Thank you to a host of colleagues, friends and family
too many to call out by name
and to
the People of our Country.

Prologue

At the time of his death on February 13, 2016, a few weeks before his eightieth birthday, Antonin Gregory Scalia had been an associate justice of the United States Supreme Court for almost thirty years. He wrote hundreds of opinions, both for the majority and in dissent. "A brief look" gives us only that – it is not really an overview, a primer, or even an introduction: all of those would likely examine more than five or six opinions.

Given the contentions in Congress regarding Scalia's replacement, it seemed a good moment to take "a brief look" at a few of the later opinions of one of this country's most vivid, passionate, and opinionated Supreme Court justices over the past 225 years.

Antonin Scalia hunted, rode elephants, sang opera, had nine children, was married to his wife for more than fifty years, and was a staunch Roman Catholic. Throughout his career, he was dedicated to the United States Constitution as written by the Founders.

He himself might have disapproved of the deadlock over the appointment of his successor. Article II, section II, of the United

Scalia: A Brief Look

States Constitution provides that the President of the United States "shall nominate, and by and with the Advice and Consent of the Senate, shall appoint ... Judges of the supreme Court ...." Not by the next President, not at some vague time in the future, not if the Senate doesn't like the current President. The members of Congress are sworn to "uphold the Constitution," and the Constitution they claim to revere says not one thing about party affiliations. For the Senate to refuse even to hear the nominee was not a possibility posed in that document on which our nation was founded.

Shortly after Justice Scalia died, political commentator David Axelrod recounted a conversation he had had some years before with Justice Scalia at a White House Correspondents dinner, when Justice David Souter had just announced his retirement. Scalia said to Axelrod, who was then a senior advisor to President Obama, "I hope [the President] sends us **someone smart.**" *(emphasis added).* Scalia went on to suggest Elena Kagan, who would be elevated to the High Court not in that round, but a year later, when another seat came vacant.[1]

Send us someone smart. Send us someone of resilient mind and firm belief in the greatness of our country in all its diversity. It is a disservice to the country, in all of its glory and in the changing world, if lawmakers only even *consider* someone who agrees with them in all things. Send us someone who can **think** – not a rubber stamp.

As many Supreme Court-watchers know, Justice Scalia's opinions make compelling reading – sometimes infuriating, sometimes amusing. Some of them are boring. (Not every case that the Supreme Court hears is equally exciting.) But Justice Scalia's opinions, whether or not one agrees with him, make one think.

---

[1] http://www.cnn.com/2016/02/14/opinions/david-axelrod-surprise-request-from-justice-scalia/ Accessed 10/22/2016

To read Justice Scalia's opinions is to watch the Constitution in action. It is testament indeed to the vision, or perhaps the flexibility, both of the Founders and of all in government who have succeeded them, that a document written more than 225 years ago as the general operating instructions for a country still works. Not that it's perfect – but it works.

Justice Scalia was an "originalist," meaning that he put his faith in the words of the original document. He looked for the interpretation that would hew most closely to what was, in his opinion, the Founders' original intent. Given that the country's issues and its technologies change over the course of time in ways that the Founders never imagined, a strictly original approach is not always possible. More than two centuries later, we cannot always divine the thinking and intent of the Framers of the Constitution.

Other commentators have observed that it is also necessary to take subsequent amendments into account. The original Framers of the Constitution provided a framework, not an immovable, once-for-all-time rule book. Ideas, technologies, and societal mores change over time, and America has changed with them. The basic framework of the U.S. Constitution remains, but each successive generation can build on that framework to meet the needs of their time.

The push-pull of the "original" viewpoint and the "living" viewpoint are indeed democracy in action. Some commentators have used the term "living originalism" to describe the melding together of the original framework and the living responses of the subsequent periods of American society as they build upon that framework. The dialogue contributes to the nation's resilience as a continuing entity, able to flex but not break under the duress of great stresses. Justice Scalia's diligence has been one factor in the dialogue, so that as the country develops, its Founders' original intents are not warped out of all recognition. And, drilling

Scalia: A Brief Look

deep, he did at times express opinions that, if even no one agreed initially, over time might be proven to be correct.

What follows is a brief look at a handful of Justice Scalia's later opinions and the issues they addressed. Normally a Supreme Court majority opinion, "the opinion of the Court," is read first, and then the dissent. Since this commentary is focused through the lens of Justice Scalia's opinions, his words will appear first, whether he wrote for the Court or in dissent. The exception will be the final case, *Glossip* v. *Gross*.

Throughout these cases, the reader will see that, while there may be clear Constitutional logic on one side or the other, the arguments of the Court and the dissent may in the end only differ by the proverbial "weight of a feather" on the scales of Justice, with concurring opinions or additional dissents bringing attention to further nuances in the discussion. Taken together, these are, indeed, our democracy in action.

Can we post the Ten Commandments in the county courthouse?

First Amendment: The separation of church and state

**McCreary County, KY, et al, v. ACLU (2005)
Scalia in dissent**

This was a case which made national news at the time, and the issue continues to resonate in some parts of the United States. Justice Scalia wrote a passionate dissent. While some of his logic cannot be faulted, the point he appears to be driving home does not always seem to answer the question. It's great reading, though – and it does make one think.

The constitutional issue

Cases which reach the Supreme Court often hinge on a question of interpretation of the United States Constitution. In this case, the issue is the Establishment Clause, a particular phrase in the First Amendment:

> "Congress shall make no law respecting an **establishment of religion**, or prohibiting the free exercise thereof; or abridging the freedom of speech, or of the press; or the right of the people peaceably to assemble, and to petition the government for a redress of grievances."

Background

When the Constitution was drafted, the founders of the young United States were very aware of where they had come from.

Scalia: A Brief Look

The English colonies had been in thrall to a powerful nation with an established national church – the Church of England. The founders (also called the Founders) were not about to have that happen again. Other clauses in the First Amendment – in the Bill of Rights as a whole, in fact – respond to other issues the colonies had had with Mother England. We'll look at some of those later. What's important here is that the Founders of the United States were not about to have a church established, promoted, or supported by the government.

Holding the line on such a pronouncement can be a little tricky sometimes – and every so often logical absurdities do arise.

This case

Two counties in Kentucky posted "large, readily visible" copies of the Ten Commandments in their courthouses:

"Thou shalt have no other gods before me.

"Thou shalt not make until thee any graven images.

"Thou shalt not take the name of the Lord thy God in vain.

"Remember the Sabbath day, to keep it holy.

"Honor thy father and thy mother.

"Thou shalt not kill.

"Thou shalt not commit adultery.

"Thou shalt not steal.

"Thou shalt not bear false witness.

"Thou shalt not covet.

"Exodus 2:03-17"

Civil rights groups, the American Civil Liberties Union (ACLU) chief among them, sued the counties for violating the Establishment Clause, and asked that the signs be taken down. (The legal term for this is an "injunction.") It *is* challenging to find a "secular purpose" for a courthouse display that begins, "Thou shalt have no other gods before me …"

The Counties tried a second time. They expanded the displays, adding several smaller signs along with the larger posting of the Commandments. Apparently that did not resolve the issue. The Commandments were still described as "distinctly religious," and the additional signs also showed religious themes and references.

On the third try, the Counties displayed nine documents of equal size, heading the display as "The Foundations of American Law and Government…," professing that the display explained the historical and legal significance not only of the Ten Commandments, but also of the Declaration of Independence, the lyrics of "The Star-Spangled Banner," and so forth. The Ten Commandments were now quoted more fully ("…for I the LORD thy God am a jealous God ….").

Justice Souter, writing for the Court, held that the **purpose** of the displays had to be considered seriously under the Establishment Clause. It did not appear that the additional documents included in the later displays were less religious in nature, and indeed the "sectarian" nature of the displays seemed to highlight monotheistic, Judeo-Christian religion.

The Founders of the United States of America did rely on "Providence," and did acknowledge a Creator. Presidents, including Abraham Lincoln, did call upon the Lord in prayer. However, the Founders did also codify the Establishment Clause in the First Amendment to the Constitution: "Congress shall make no law respecting an establishment of religion…." If documents are posted in the halls of the county courthouse, their very

Scalia: A Brief Look

placement implies that the government has endorsed their message. So there is a fine line between a person's expression of faith and the government pronouncing (establishing) the faith of the country. The Court noted that the benchmark was a government mandate of neutrality, whether between the beliefs of several religions, or between religious beliefs and the beliefs of the nonreligious.

So that is the core argument: **Official Religious Neutrality**. Ours is not an atheistic society – that is, a society believing that there is no deity – but a society that is officially neutral on the subject, because its people, in all their diversity, hold differing views on religion.

This Court's opinion emphasized the need for religious tolerance, a tolerance reached as the outcome of the founders' experience with various religious wars. A nation which values stability and liberty needs to founded on respect for the views of all of its members, not only on a majority belief.

Consider religious wars from the time of England's House of Tudor, when England's King Henry VIII first split his country's church from the established church of Rome, all the way to those war-torn regions of the Middle East in the early 21st century, where the core issue, yet again, is religion. You, the 21st century reader, then see what the Founders were trying to avoid, and what the issue at hand is now. Posting the Ten Commandments in the courthouse in this instance may have seemed, to some, like a step at the top of a very slippery slope.

Justice Scalia's dissent noted that religious tolerance does not equate with the complete prohibition of public religious expression. The writers of the Constitution "believed that morality was essential to the well-being of society and that religion was the best way to foster morality." All well and good. The basic morality set forth in the Decalogue -- not to steal, murder, and covet one's neighbor's family or possessions – is indeed a foundation of societal tenets: those things that everyone, no matter their beliefs, considers to be taboo. But this does not hold equally for *all* of these commandments. For example, adultery and swearing, while forbidden, are practiced widely (more widely than murder, at least); covetousness of one's neighbor's possessions may be taboo, but covetousness is, subtly or not, foundational to consumerism and advertising. Honoring one's parents, while at times the bane of the forgetful or self-serving offspring, might be dangerous if the parent to be honored in fact abuses the child.

But there also appears to be some contention regarding the placement of the displays. Is it really acceptable to expect that someone who disagrees will turn their back on the displays? Is there an acceptable translation of the Ten Commandments? The King James translation, although familiar to many, comes from a Protestant Christian translation of the Bible.

Justice Scalia found that even an isolated display of the Decalogue would have been "at worst" equivocal, perhaps showing respect for Judaism, or for law in general. But such thinking appears difficult to equate with "I the LORD thy God am a jealous God..." These are the Commandments of God, and seem unequivocal in that message. In attempting to justify their posting as a secular message, Justice Scalia appeared to water down the significance of their message.

Justice Scalia's dissent spent many column-inches disputing Justice Stevens' dissent in *Van Orden v. Perry* (2005), an opinion handed down the same day as *McCreary County*. *Van Orden* was another Establishment Clause case, which dealt with a display of the Ten Commandments on the grounds of the Texas State House, first erected in the early 1960s but apparently unchallenged for some decades. In that case, the Court affirmed the secular purpose of that display. Justice Scalia joined in that opinion.

In his own concurrence in *Van Orden* v. *Perry,* Justice Scalia expressed a preference for honoring the Ten Commandments in a manner not calculated to convert the onlooker. That might have been the situation in *Van Orden* but, on the available evidence, appeared not to be the case in *McCreary County*.

Justice Breyer, in his concurring opinion in *Van Orden*, contrasted that case with *McCreary County*. He noted the religious elements of the displays and their potential effect on the viewer. That might indicate a governmental effort to promote religion, and not simply an effort to reflect, historically, the secular impact of a religiously-inspired document. Further, a recent display, mounted by a government, might have a different effect than a "long-standing, pre-existing" monument might have.

In his *McCreary County* dissent, Justice Scalia likened the display of the Ten Commandments to the inclusion of religious elements in a holiday display. But if that were the case, it is unlikely that quite so much passion would be in evidence in court cases involving the display of the Ten Commandments. The Ten Commandments, as a foundational document, do carry more weight than many a symbol of a holiday.

For many of that monotheistic 97% of Americans, in particular for many believing Christians, the Commandments as an object of reverence might be on a par only with the Cross. And although Justice Scalia brushed aside doctrinal differences between the variations on the Decalogue as seen by the various monotheistic faiths, one cannot help but observe that clearly they are important to many, even if such differences were not important to *him*.

Justice Scalia seemed to find that, if a certain translation of the Ten Commandments is acceptable to 97% of the population, than it may be posted in the courthouse. Given the importance of the Ten Commandments as expressions of faith to a large segment of the population, it may indeed seem weak or ineffectual to place such a high emphasis on refraining from including them in a government display. But, as Justice O'Connor observed in her concurring opinion, the goal of the religion clauses in the First

Church and state?

Amendment is clearly to continue to preserve religious liberty, particularly when we see the results, elsewhere in the world, of the violence caused by governments exercising religious authority.

To read the several opinions in *McCreary County* and *Van Orden* is, as mentioned earlier, to watch democracy in action. These issues have resonated throughout this nation's history. Divergent opinions are held not only by Supreme Court Justices but by citizens of the country as a whole. These ongoing discussions are our country at work, as We the People of the United States of America wrestle with issues which, as they recur, allow us to develop our thought – as individuals and as a nation – regarding religion and faith; race, gender, and human equality; interpersonal relations and marriage; privacy as affected by changing technologies, and a host of others.

Maybe the religious significance of the McCreary County posters could be ignored by the viewer. Certainly, many of this country's founders, subsequent presidents and leaders did invoke the Creator, a monotheistic God. It was also true that the Ten Commandments are one of the foundations of this country's legal beliefs. But a heightened religious effect may change the point of view: What weight is the viewer supposed to assign to such a display?

One image that is used by judges instructing juries, as well as by counsel (defense and prosecution) pleading for their clients, is the image of the feather. Weigh the evidence presented to you, jury, and if one side or the other tips the scales of justice *by even so much as the weight of a feather*, you must decide the case accordingly.

In *McCreary County v. ACLU,* there are arguments to be made on both sides. However, the feather rests on the scale of the Court's opinion. **Official Religious Neutrality**. It may be merely the weight of a feather. But the McCreary County display might affect the viewer more powerfully than the Texas State House display in *Van Orden,* if only because a hallway is a narrow corridor, where an outdoor display is not.

What if the Foundations Displays had presented a different translation? Not the King James translation familiar to so many Protestant Christians, but a translation from a Roman Catholic Bible, a Jewish translation of the Torah, or a translation from the Islamic Qur'an? Would citizens have been outraged that the government appeared to be promoting that particular faith?

All three faiths – Jewish, Christian, and Islam – do come from the same roots. But there are differences among translations, and about what the "ten" commandments are counted summarize. For example, the Qu'ran posts the concepts contained in the Ten Commandments without quoting that specific list. Had the Counties in this case posted "values to live by" without citing or quoting one particular list or a translation from a religious text, perhaps the case might have proceeded differently.

Would such a list have had the same impact?

"Who is 'my neighbor'?"

The Second Amendment:
Keeping a handgun for self-defense

D.C. v. *Heller* (2008)
Scalia for the Court

The United States of America may be one of the most violent of the so-called "developed" countries of the world, and also one of the most racially divided. That some of the populace finds it "necessary" to keep handguns may or may not be unusual among developed nations. Three opinions are here: Justice Scalia "for the Court" – the majority opinion, joined by Chief Justice Roberts and Justices Kennedy, Thomas and Alito – and Justices Stephens and Breyer in two dissenting opinions, each joined by the other and by Justices Souter and Ginsburg. The reasoning of the Framers of the Constitution, as interpreted by the members of the current Supreme Court, might in fact lead to a viewpoint which this majority would prefer, rather than what the Framers originally intended.

Once again, there is a featherweight on the scales of Justice. The net result of the opinions is that, despite best efforts, an attempted "originalist" interpretation of the Constitution may actually have resulted in a changed interpretation – a "living" interpretation.

Scalia: A Brief Look

In the U.S. Constitution's Second Amendment, the concept that "the people had the right to keep and bear Arms" did not mean that "the people" had the right to blow away their neighbors. In the late 18th century, when the Constitution was drafted, guns were primarily for military use and for hunting for food – the latter not a use necessary in urban areas in the 21st century. And it seems unlikely that the Founders of this country were particularly worried about safeguarding "sportsmanship." The Founders were very aware of their recent history, wherein their former rulers in England had embargoed gunpowder and attempted to confiscate arms in order to limit the colonists' effective resistance.

Although the logic of the opinion of the Court, and Justice Scalia, appears to hang together, it is difficult to tell whether or not the net result was in fact the one which the Court's majority expected.

The constitutional issue

The issue hinges on the interpretation of the Second Amendment to the U. S. Constitution, which reads: "A well regulated Militia, being necessary to the security of a free State, the right of the people to keep and bear Arms, shall not be infringed."

Looking back from the early 21st century, we see several questions of interpretation. Did the Framers mean that the right of the people "to keep and bear Arms" was specifically in support of having a "well regulated Militia, being necessary to the security of a free State"? Or did they mean that the people had the right to keep arms for *whatever* purpose, and that the establishment and maintenance of a well-regulated militia, although necessary to the security of the State, was separate from the right of the people to keep arms? And what were "Arms," exactly, and what did it mean to "bear" them?

Background

The District of Columbia had a ban on the private ownership of handguns under its Firearms Control Regulation Act of 1975. That Act banned not only handguns but also automatic weapons, and also the ownership of any unlicensed weapons. Exceptions included ownership by police officers, and guns registered before 1975. Also, any weapon kept at home was to either be unloaded or to have a trigger lock or similar disabling device. The District's regulations were among the strictest in the nation, but it is worth bearing in mind that, unlike any of the States, the District of Columbia encompasses only 61.4 square miles in area and is entirely urban.

Respondent Dick Heller, a 66-year-old D.C. special police officer, was licensed to carry a weapon while on duty. He applied for a license to be able to keep a loaded handgun in his home. The District refused. Heller, as one of a group of plaintiffs, filed suit in Federal District Court on Second Amendment grounds. The District Court dismissed the complaint, and the Court of Appeals reversed. The case next went to the Supreme Court.

Apparently the case was searched out and funded by an independent party, a former resident of the District in whose view the D.C. law infringed on citizens' liberties. Not that he owned, or wished to own, a gun himself, but he had the personal funds with which to recruit plaintiffs and hire legal counsel. Is this a fair activity as a citizen, in order to improve a city and a society, or a rich person's attempt to shape the city-society to his own theoretical ends?

This case

The opinion of the Court, delivered by Justice Scalia, began with a parsing of the "prefatory" and "operative" clauses of the Second Amendment. That is, respectively, "A well regulated Militia, being necessary to the security of a free State" and "the right of the people to keep and bear arms shall not be infringed." The majority, examining the operative clause first, emphasized the interpretation of the phrases "the people," "to keep," and to "bear arms." It focused at length on the right to keep arms for self-

Scalia: A Brief Look

defense purposes.

The Court did, however, note that this was not a right to keep *any* arms for any and all purposes. While not limiting its Second Amendment interpretation to 18th-century weaponry, it also did not broaden the scope to include, for example, sawed-off shotguns or automatic/semi-automatic weapons.

After all these years, it is difficult to state unequivocally what the Founders intended, despite the attempt of some members of the 21st-century Court to adhere closely to an "originalist" interpretation of the Constitution. There are now also constitutional scholars and journalists who point out that the Constitution, as it now stands, must encompass all of its Amendments, not only the Constitution of the late eighteenth century. If the Founders meant to protect self-defense or sport shooting but did not explicitly state that, how are we to interpret that intention at the beginning of the 21st century? Which resources, contemporaneous with the drafting of the Constitution, might be relied on? In the *Heller* opinions, tens of pages are devoted to the comparison and contrasting of early sources, as if a hefty weight of minutiae might serve to tip the balance.

There are certain activities which may be so common in a society that they go without saying. No one may think to codify a right if it is nearly universal in a society, such as the right to keep arms for hunting, or a right to keep an automobile or a smart phone. The right may be codified if it is endangered, such as the right to "keep and bear Arms" if a government has tried to disarm a populace.

But some decades or centuries hence, later generations may question: Why did their forebears did not codify the right to own a smart phone – were they not invented yet? Or were they in such widespread and largely benign use that of course a smart phone was permissible, and that "right" need not be set down in a written Bill of Rights?

The opinion of the Court also examined some nineteenth-century case law and legislation. It cited an 1829 decision by Michigan's Supreme Court which found that citizens had the right to keep and bear arms, although not for unlawful or unjustifiable purpose[s]," such as destroying one's neighbor. The Court also discussed post-Civil War legislation regarding black citizens' constitutional right to bear arms and the attempts prevalent in some Southern states to deny blacks that right, also noting the controversy as to whether or not the Second Amendment addressed any entity other than the federal government itself. There seemed to be further difference of opinion as to whether the Amendment in question was the Second or the Fourteenth. The Court made all of these observations in the context of bearing arms for military purposes.

The majority opinion noted that a "militia" in the 18th century, when the Bill of Rights was ratified, was the body of all citizens capable of military service, who would bring to militia duty the sorts of lawful weapons that they possessed at home. In the 21st century, an effective home militia might require sophisticated arms that are highly unusual in society at large. Indeed, it may be true that no amount of small arms could be useful against modern-day bombers and tanks.

The majority, having reasoned its way through those historical precedents it found applicable, arrived at the present case. But a reader following the majority's logic might gain the uncomfortable sense that the Court's majority was attempting to, in the old phrase, put new wine into old wineskins (which, by the way, burst when reused).

The majority made a bid for the advantages of handgun ownership. The reasons enumerated may all be true (and the dissenting opinions also weigh in regarding these attributes), but some phrases sound nearly like advertising slogans, as in, "the American people have considered the handgun to be the quintessential self-defense weapon..." and "...the most popular weapon chosen by Americans for self-defense in the home...."

Scalia: A Brief Look

The majority held that the District of Columbia's ban on handgun possession in the home violated the Second Amendment, as did the District's ban on allowing the firearm to be stored in a manner "operable for the purpose of immediate self-defense" – that is, loaded and not locked. Although the majority took note of gun violence as a problem in the United States, nevertheless it held that it was not the Supreme Court's role "to pronounce the Second Amendment extinct." Which is true, but what or who did the Court's majority interpret the Second Amendment to protect? And from whom?

In his dissenting opinion, Justice John Paul Stevens examined the prefatory statement. He found it to indicate that the Amendment's primary purpose was militia-related. He noted that the Court's opinion did not present evidence supporting congressional regulation of weapons as used by civilians. Several of the States had such language in their own declarations of rights, but by and large such regulation *was* left to the States.

Here we see the impact of a conundrum presented by the nature of the District of Columbia. As a jurisdiction under direct federal governance and not a part of any of the several States, the District's regulations rise to the level of the Supreme Court rather more quickly that would occur had the plaintiffs in question been resident in, perhaps, a county in nearby Maryland or Virginia. There, such a lawsuit would work first through the judiciary of the home state.

Justice Stevens' dissent took issue with the Court's method of interpretation in highlighting the "operative phrase" separate from the "prefatory phrase." The Court's method might be likened to discussing an object ahead of, or separate from, that which powers it, (or a colloquial paraphrase, discussing the cart before the horse). Justice Stevens' dissent highlighted the historical context of the Framers' concerns regarding permitting the existence of a national standing army *without* the balance of state militias. It noted the lack of a specific indication that the Framers intended to address the right of self-defense in the Second

Amendment, and subsequent commentators have also taken issue with that position. In sum, the dissent found the majority's opinion to be weak and somewhat stretched. Subsequent commentators have found the right of self-defense elsewhere in the constitutional amendments – but not in the Second Amendment.

The dissent began with an examination of the preamble to the Second Amendment, recognizing the importance of a "well regulated" militia, and examining several states' Declarations of Rights from that time. It noted that the Second Amendment did *not* mention the right to use firearms for hunting or personal self-defense, although several states had done so in their own Declarations of Rights. It also quoted the seminal text of *Marbury v. Madison* (1803) regarding interpretation of the Constitution: "It cannot be presumed that any clause in the constitution is intended to be without effect." The dissent further noted that the Supreme Court does *not* ordinarily interpret an operative clause out of the context of its preamble, as the Court attempted to do here in this case when it downplayed the importance of the prefatory clause of the Second Amendment.

This dissent took a different stance from the Court regarding both the interpretation and the means of interpreting the Second Amendment clauses. It pointed to the Court's handling of some of its authorities and sources, as when the Court invoked Blackstone's *Commentaries on the Laws of England* (published in the late 1760s) as a "preeminent authority" while at the same time the Court disregarded Blackstone's means of interpretation. Justice Stevens's dissent also turned its attention to Justice Joseph Story's 1833 *Commentaries on the Constitution of the United States* – where, again, the interpretations by this case's majority and dissent differed.

In reviewing the post-Civil War legislation brought forth by the Court's opinion, Justice Stevens's dissent then pointed out that such statements cannot be used as proof of the original intent of the Constitution, having been made long after the Amendment was framed. The Court stated that blacks were not being prohibited from carrying arms in an organized state militia, but the sources from the time which it used to support that statement, unfortunately might indeed have referred to such disarmament.

Justice Stevens's dissent went on to consider interpretations of earlier Supreme Court case law and their holdings on the Second Amendment's application either to state governments or private citizens, as opposed to its application to the federal government and organized militias. The dissent concluded that "the right the Court announces was not 'enshrined' in the Second Amendment by the Framers; it is the product of today's law-changing decision, without textual or historical background to bolster 'the right of law-abiding, responsible citizens to use firearms in defense of hearth and home' elevated above other interests in the Second Amendment." (Do we, the People – not the Supreme Court – still refer to "the defense of hearth and home"? Consider that many of us now have central heating.)

The Court appeared to argue that the Framers had authorized future generations to define contemporary gun control policy on a case by case basis, although there was no evidence in the majority opinion to support what it referred to as "judicial lawmaking." But have we not been made aware, in other contexts, of a preference for the legislators, not the judiciary, to make laws?

In his dissenting opinion, Justice Stephen A. Breyer found that the District of Columbia's law was consistent with the Second Amendment. The District's parameters met the needs of urban crime – a problem which covered a local scope, a limited area, and considered a weapon favored by armed criminals in that area.

Justice Breyer's dissent enumerated colonial examples of gun regulations then thought to be in harmony with the "right to keep and bear arms." Included were regulations in certain urban areas, such as Boston, New York and Philadelphia, which each tailored their regulations to their own requirements. None of the dissent's evidence supported a right to keep a gun at home in order to shoot burglars. Despite the majority's derision of what it termed an "interest-balancing" inquiry, those interests bring back once more our image of the featherweight and its effect on the balance-scales of justice. On the one hand, gun use is protected by the Second Amendment; on the other hand, legislation responds to local governments' public safety concerns.

Justice Breyer's dissent reviewed the legislative history and supporting statistics leading to the enactment of the District's firearms control law. It included not only the number of gun-related deaths in this country each day and each year, but also the percentage which was accidental, and the number of those which involved children. This dissent highlighted the involvement of firearms both in deaths and violent acts among people known to each other as opposed to premeditated criminal acts, and also in incidents of spontaneous violence due to passion, anger, or intoxication.

The dissent stressed that while a handgun might be useful in home protection against an intruder, such accessibility and ease of use also made it vulnerable to use against family members or other relatives or in suicides, and available to fall into the hands of children. While shootings appeared to be much more of an issue in urban areas, whether or not handguns were legally available did not seem to correlate directly. Further, a ban on handguns also did not appear to correlate directly to a decrease in violent crime. In other words, handguns that were either registered with the District before the 1975 ban, brought from neighboring states (legally or not), or otherwise obtained illegally, were used in the commission of such crimes: the ban could not be shown to be a deterrent.

On the face of it, a ban on handguns might appear to equate to a decrease in crime (fewer guns = less crime), but in reality that did not seem to be the case. In fact, it might appear that the known presence of handguns in a location would act as a crime deterrent to intrusion and crime. If it were only that simple! The dissent outlined other uses to which that handgun might be put:

family homicide, suicide, violence involving children, and the random murder of suspected intruders who are not true intruders.

This dissent also noted a reverse correlation between strict gun laws and high crime rates existed in foreign nations. But a Constitutional ban would remove from states and local jurisdictions even the option to tailor the law to a particular, local situation. The United States are now geographically too large and too diverse for a "one-size-fits-all" approach to such an issue. Local knowledge and local solutions must be taken into account.

The dissent also noted that, had the Framers focused on any self-defense interest, urban crime would not have been a central issue. Rebellions, frontier defense, and crime while traveling would likely have been more prevalent than the consideration of rights in urban settings. Furthermore, "handguns" at the time would have not had the same convenience and utility as 21st-century weaponry.

In the wake of the *Heller* decision, there have been numerous challenges to gun laws in the lower courts. Many courts have turned back such cases, and many jurists have referenced Justice Scalia's own words in the *Heller* majority opinion: "the right secured by the Second Amendment is not unlimited." Also, in the wake of horrific multiple murders, it is clear that the existing law does not keep weapons out the hands of mass murderers, and loosening laws to allow more guns onto the streets will not necessarily make our country safer, but merely heighten a perception of security.

"One nation"?

Article I, section 8:
"Uniform Naturalization" v. States' sovereignty

Arizona v. U.S. (2012)
Scalia concurred in part and dissented in part

Arizona's southern boundary forms part of the United States' border with Mexico. Along with the borders of Texas, New Mexico and California, it is subject to many attempted crossings by Mexican nationals and others seeking to enter the United States illegally. Many die due to exposure to heat or cold, drowning, traffic accidents and other means. The United States Border Patrol is responsible for the nearly 2,000-mile stretch, using fences, drones, guns and other methods of protection. An additional wall, touted by some office-seekers, would not change the equation. Tunnels have already been attempted under existing barriers.

Concerned that other, more populous states were receiving more federal resources for border protection, Arizona in 2010 enacted a bill providing expanded powers to its own law enforcement, in order to provide for increased policing of suspected illegal aliens in Arizona, and to allow Arizona law enforcement to expel "undesirables."

Simple, right? Not really. This is not a matter of keeping the citizens of another state out of Arizona, but the nationals of another country out of the United States. That is a power which has been left to the Federal Government.

The constitutional issue

In the United States Constitution (Article I, section 8, clauses 1, 2, and 4), "The Congress shall have power ... to provide for the common defence and general welfare of the United States ... to regulate commerce with foreign nations ... to establish a uniform rule of naturalization ...." Further, the Constitution's "Supremacy Clause" (Article 6, clause 2) established that Federal law takes precedence over State law. "This Constitution, and the Laws of the United States which shall be made in Pursuance thereof; and all Treaties made, or which shall be made, under the Authority of the United States, shall be the supreme Law of the Land; and the Judges in every State shall be bound thereby, any Thing in the Constitution or Laws of any State to the Contrary notwithstanding."

In short, federal law takes precedence over state law. It is for the *federal* government to interact with other nations.

This case

Justice Kennedy delivered the opinion of the Court, joined by Chief Justice Roberts and Justices Ginsburg, Breyer and Sotomayor. Justices Scalia, Thomas, and Alito each wrote a separate opinion, and each concurred in part and dissented in part. Justice Kagan took no part in the deliberations: she had acted as Solicitor General of the United States before she was appointed to the Court.

As was usual for him, Justice Scalia looked to his understanding of the "original" meaning of the Constitution when expressing his opinion. He emphasized the United States as an indivisible "Union of sovereign states," (emphasis on the States' sovereignty). He saw the opinion of the Court in *Arizona v United States* as "depriv[ing] States of ... the power to exclude from the sovereign's territory people who have no right to be there." This he saw as an essential right of sovereignty, and he posited that Arizona's right in this matter was "subject only to those limitations expressed in the Constitution or constitutionally imposed by Congress." But that limitation *is* expressed in the Constitution, and a State is not the same as a gated community. The United States Congress, in setting forth the Immigration and Naturalization Law, had taken on the primary responsibility for immigration policy. So, to quote a 1758 treatise on the Law of Nations, as Justice Scalia did, is no longer entirely useful. This is a union of States, not of individual nations.

Justice Scalia quoted earlier opinions of the Supreme Court, which saw the exclusion of foreigners by a sovereign nation as "an accepted maxim of international law." But having accepted the modern prevalence of federal immigration limits, Justice Scalia reverted to an emphasis on the traditional role of the states to regulate immigration. He acknowledged that, under the U.S. Constitution, federal law and regulation takes precedence over state regulations. And he stressed the fact that, unlike regulations for more minor issues such as (he suggests) bubble-gum advertising, this federal law "go[es] to the *core* of state sovereignty".

"Even in its international relations, the Federal Government must live with the inconvenient fact that it is a Union of independent States, who have their own sovereign powers," stated Justice Scalia.

But likewise, the States must live with the oft-times extremely inconvenient fact that **they are a Union.** We have seen this conundrum time and again over the course of the Nation's history, as the States wrestle with such far-reaching issues as definitions of who one may marry, or regarding the enslavement of other

Scalia: A Brief Look

humans.

As Justice Scalia noted, the issue in this case was whether or not Arizona law and federal law were in conflict, if Arizona sought to exclude those the federal government would admit, or admit those the federal law would exclude. In his opinion, the Arizona law at issue applied to aliens who, while not removed by authority of the federal government, also did not have the privilege of being present under that law.

In his view, Arizona was entitled to its own immigration policy, so long as that does not conflict with federal law – even if it were more *rigorous* than federal law. But we see this disparity in other states as well, with other issues: can Vermont, for example, have more detailed labeling of generic pharmaceuticals and genetically modified foods than is mandated by the federal Food and Drug Administration? Again, federal law trumps state law.

Justice Scalia in this case quoted the opinion of the Court as saying, "it is not a crime for a removable alien to remain present in the United States." And he continued: "It is not a federal crime, to be sure. But there is no reason Arizona cannot make it a state crime for a removable alien (or any illegal alien, for that matter), to remain present in Arizona."

Here we see one of the age-old arguments of the Nation: where does the federal law take precedence, and where do the States' individual rights prevail? Perhaps the most long-standing example, for this country, came to a head in the 1860s, in the War Between the States – although that series of bloody confrontations unfortunately cannot be said to have settled the matter.

One also sees the specter of "No Irish (or Italians) Need Apply...." How does that attitude differ from the underlying attitude in Arizona's proposed law, except in the skin color of the targeted immigration group?

Would this case be clearer if the state border in question was not also a national border? If we were discussing, perhaps, Colorado or Utah, entirely surrounded by other States, rather than a State such as Arizona (or, presumably, Montana) bordered on one side by a foreign ("alien") nation?

Justice Scalia's opinion advocated the removal of "unlawfully present aliens," no matter what. "Arizona is entitled to … *at least* bring them to federal officials' attention, which is all that [the state law at issue] necessarily entails. (In my view [Scalia's], the State can go further than this, and punish them for their unlawful entry and presence in Arizona." Furthermore, "the State's whole complaint – the reason this law was passed and this case has arisen—is that the citizens of Arizona believe federal priorities are too lax. The State has the sovereign power to protect its borders more rigorously if it wishes, absent any valid federal prohibition."

But is the federal reasoning for not detaining or deporting certain aliens a "valid" prohibition? Or, if the reasoning is simply a lack of federal resources, would perhaps Arizona, and like-minded states, be willing for the Nation to deploy national resources not, say, in Afghanistan or Syria, but rather in Arizona? The federal financial pie is not infinite, after all. To shift funding from overseas policing to home border protection, rather than from other domestic programs such as the funding of education or Social Security, seems a wiser allocation of the Nation's resources.

Justice Scalia quoted an earlier Supreme Court opinion, *Plyler v. Doe* (1982), to support the concept that the States are not completely powerless regarding illegal immigration, particularly when an influx might have a "discernable impact" on state resources. That may hold in this case as well. Justice Scalia referenced Arizona's need to protect, for one, its unemployment benefits system. He further highlighted the potential that the punishment for a violation of state law might exceed that for a violation of federal law, and mentions (although without examples) that state penalties for the sale of illegal drugs might exceed

Scalia: A Brief Look

federal penalties.

"It holds no fear for me, as it does for the Court," Justice Scalia intoned, "that exercise of State power might in some circumstances 'frustrate' federal policies." As presented – whether or not this was Justice Scalia's intent – this seems to imply that a State would not *care* if it frustrated a federal policy, whether or not that policy might work to the State's advantage in the long term.

At the same time, Scalia continued with a very valid observation: "What I do fear – and what Arizona and the States that support it fear – is that 'federal policies' of non-enforcement will leave the States helpless before those evil effects of illegal immigration that the Court's opinion dutifully recites in its prologue but leaves un-remedied in its disposition." Several pages further into his opinion, Justice Scalia expanded on this: "[T]here is no reason why the Federal Executive's need to allocate *its* scarce enforcement resources should disable Arizona from devoting *its* resources to illegal immigration in Arizona that in its view the Federal Executive has given short shrift."

Again, a valid viewpoint. Would it not be possible to find a compromise, or common ground, on which to work this out? For this is the core of the matter: a problem exists which the federal government cannot handle equitably across the entire stretch of territory to be protected, and so its resources are focused on California and Texas. Arizona sees that, and is willing to step up to assist.

The Federal government's concerns include (a) the protection of its own powers, and (b) that the State(s) not jeopardize any ongoing federal investigations OR (c) overstep the enforcement measures established by the federal government. In assisting the Federal Government's efforts, it would be the *State's* responsibility *not* to set up its own police state, so to speak. As one example, the Nation saw this during some of the civil rights disputes in the American South in the mid-twentieth century.

One can understand the Federal Government's reluctance to permit sufficient State power that might lead to *that* sort of action again. Once again, in light of the nation's history, one understands the cautious approach to a seemingly minor detail, which has the potential to be the first step at the top of a slippery slope. In the late Justice's inimitable fashion, he returned the question to a historical-constitutional viewpoint. He noted the States' "jealousy ... with regard to their sovereignty" at the time of the 1787 Constitutional Convention. Well and good – but he then noted, further, "as reflected in the innumerable proposals that never left Independence Hall." If that were the case, why bring it up now? That is an example of delving into the legislative history that brings a law to fruition: a method of research that, in many circumstances, Justice Scalia repudiated.

While it may be amusing to speculate on what the Framers of the Constitution *might* have done, or *might* have thought, in the end that is speculation in alternative history. That is not the Constitution as it was written and approved; that is not the Nation we have now.

It is perhaps ironic that Justice Scalia was willing in this case to call out the "very human realities that gave rise to the suit", and to reference the plight of the Arizona citizens who "feel themselves under siege by large numbers of illegal immigrants who invade their property, strain their social services, ... place their lives in jeopardy [and] compete openly with Arizona citizens for employment."

Why was this an issue in Arizona? Why not also in the cities of the urban northeast, where immigrants from the Caribbean islands and various parts of Asia may strain social services and compete openly with this nation's citizens for employment? Was it because the immigrants are competing with American citizens who also have dark skins? Or because this is not, in fact, part of the values on which our nation was founded?

Scalia: A Brief Look

The opinion of the Court, the majority opinion, was delivered by Justice Kennedy, joined by Chief Justice Roberts and Justices Ginsburg, Breyer, and Sotomayor.

The opinion of the Court set out the fundamental federal powers to determine immigration policy, which has wide-reaching (that is, national) impact affecting trade, tourism, investments and diplomatic relations. Foreign countries, not surprisingly, ought to be able to interact with a national sovereignty regarding their own nationals, not treat with fifty separate States. The Court quotes *The Federalist*, noting that "bordering States ... might take action that would undermine foreign relations." If one is reaching back to the 1780s for a supporting, founding document, one need not look farther than *The Federalist* in attempting to divine the thought and purposes of the Constitution's Framers.

The Court's opinion further detailed the requirements and specifications set forth by Congress concerning the responsibilities of, and treatment of, noncitizens present here in the United States – including the circumstances under which they might be removed. "Unauthorized workers trying to support their families, for example, likely pose less danger than alien smugglers, or aliens who commit a serious crime[, and...] an individual case may turn on many factors..." such as children born in this country, a record of distinguished military service, or long ties to the community. Removal from this nation might also be inadvisable due to factors in the alien's native country such as civil war or political persecution. Despite such circumstances, the Court cited 2010 statistics totaling some hundreds of thousands of aliens who were removed from this nation by the Federal Government.

The Court did note that, by one estimate unauthorized aliens comprise six percent of Arizona's population and, in populous areas, might perpetrate a statistically disproportionate percentage of serious crime. Arizona's issues ought not to be underestimated or brushed aside. Having set that background, the Court addressed the potential for conflict, or cross-purposes, if there were not a clear rule for national and state sovereignties. The Court pointed out, once again, that the Supremacy Clause provides a clear rule that federal law "shall be the supreme Law of the Land ..." The Court traced the history of federal law, and case law, in developing the nation's immigration and refugee policy as it stands today. It concluded that the framework of the Immigration Reform and Control Act of 1986 reflected an intent not to criminalize unauthorized aliens without cause: such actions would conflict with the federal government's policy and objectives. In considering the details of the Arizona state law, the Court expressed concern that, if a State implemented an immigration policy separate from that of the federal government, there might well be a danger of harassment of, perhaps, a veteran, college student, or someone assisting with a criminal investigation whom federal officials had determined should not be removed.

In general terms, there we have it. The Court observed that "Immigration policy shapes the destiny of the Nation." The talents and contributions of those who have made their way across deserts or oceans to reach the United States are foundational to this country. Although "Arizona may have understandable frustrations with the problems caused by illegal immigration ... the State may not pursue policies that undermine federal law."

Yet ongoing dialogue remains necessary: Building a wall, or other draconian measures, will not be the solution any more than such measures have been curative in ages past. And many incoming immigrants provide hard work, ideas and services which earlier generations cannot or can no longer provide: this is, after all, a *nation* of immigrants. The Founders themselves were immigrants on these shores. Twenty-first century Americans, if we have forgotten, would do well to remember that.

What's "unreasonable" searching in the 21st century?

The Fourth Amendment and developing technologies

***United States* v. *Jones* (2012)**
(use of GPS tracking device)
Scalia for the Court

***Maryland* v. *King* (2013)**
(DNA ID)
Scalia in dissent

***Florida* v. *Jardines* (2013)**
(narcotics dog)
Scalia for the Court

Here we consider a trio of Fourth Amendment cases from 2012 and 2013. For *United States v. Jones* and for *Florida v. Jardines*, Justice Scalia wrote the opinion of the Court; for *Maryland v. King*, he was in dissent.

The constitutional issue

The Fourth Amendment to the Constitution declares that "the right of the people to be secure in their persons, houses, papers, and effects, against unreasonable searches and seizures, shall not be violated, and no Warrants shall issue, but upon probable cause, supported by Oath or affirmation, and particularly describing the place to be searched, and the persons or things to be seized." Although the general concept has held over time, the technologies and nuances of the 21st century are often ones which the Framers may not have envisioned in the 18th century. The general question becomes: What level of privacy can the people reasonably expect in the 21st century? Are there still any relevant analogies from 18th-century life?

Let us consider each case in turn.

In *U.S. v. Jones,* the government obtained a warrant permitting the installation of a GPS (global positioning system) device on a vehicle used exclusively by Jones. (As it happened, the device was installed neither within the time period nor in the geographic location indicated in the warrant.) The device tracked the movements of the vehicle for 28 days, after which time Jones and others were indicted on charges of drug trafficking.

Justice Scalia delivered the opinion of the Court. He was joined by Chief Justice Roberts and Justices Kennedy, Thomas and Sotomayor. The opinion held that the Government's attachment of the GPS to the vehicle, and its use of that GPS to monitor the vehicle's movements, did constitute a "search" under the Fourth Amendment.

Justice Sotomayor also filed a concurring opinion. Justice Alito filed an opinion "concurring in the judgment," in which Justices Ginsburg, Breyer and Kagan joined.

In the majority opinion, the Court held that the Government, by installing a GPS device on the respondent's vehicle, implemented a "search." The Court did not doubt that such a physical "intrusion" would have been considered a search "within the meaning of the Fourth Amendment when it was adopted." The

Scalia: A Brief Look

Government maintained that there was no search, and that, driving a vehicle on public streets, Jones could not reasonably expect the vehicle was private.

But for most of the Nation's history the Fourth Amendment was understood to be concerned with government trespass on a person's body, house, papers, and effects. And Jones's vehicle certainly counted as an "effect." Justice Scalia, writing for the Court, emphasized that, in applying the 18th-century guarantee against unreasonable searches, the Court intended to provide at *least* the same degree of protection that was afforded at the time the Amendment was first adopted. Justice Scalia noted a concern about the constitutionality of achieving such data-gathering by electronic means without physically invading someone's privacy; but since that concern was not part of the case in *U.S. v. Jones*, the Court did not address that issue in its opinion.

But hold that thought, as technology continues to evolve.

Justice Sotomayor's concurring opinion carried the point further, noting that where surveillance did not require invasion on property, the "trespassory test" invoked by the majority might not provide guidance. She further noted that GPS surveillance had "unique attributes" which might require further legal attention, since a GPS had the capability to provide data about a person's movements, including visits to medical facilities, or places of entertainment or social gathering, such that unchecked government data collection and storage might lead to the sort of abuse seen in non-democratic societies.

Justice Alito's opinion, while concurring in the Court's judgment, found that the Court strained its Fourth-Amendment interpretation through its focus on 18th-century law. In a footnote, Justice Scalia had suggested an 18th-century analogy to the GPS – a constable conducting surveillance by concealing himself in the target's coach. But the analogy does seem somewhat strained to a 21st century questioner: "How big was the constable? How big was the coach? Did this occur in daylight or at night How far was the constable able to travel before he was discovered?"

The tort, or wrong, was the intrusion on an individual's privacy, whether or not physical entry occurred. Justice Alito's concurrence further touched upon not only "disharmony" but also several concerns he noted in the majority's approach in this case. Since several other justices joined with Justice Alito but *not* with the opinion of the Court, one can surmise that fully four justices might have been in agreement with the final outcome but not with Justice Scalia's reasoning, which, Justice Alito had found might lead to "incongruous" results.

Developing technologies might provide increased convenience or security at the expense of privacy, and many people may find the tradeoff worthwhile. Justice Alito observed that dramatic technological change may lead to periods in which popular expectations are in flux, and significant changes in popular attitudes may occur after a time. Even if the public does not welcome the diminution of privacy, they may eventually reconcile themselves to this development as inevitable.

At the same time, concern about new intrusions on privacy may spur the enactment of legislative protections. This is what ultimately happened with respect to wiretapping. Faced with such a time of change, Justice Alito and his concurring justices saw a society in flux: the concurring opinion called on Congress to address the lack of legislation to regulate the use of GPS technology for law enforcement purposes.

As we review two more Fourth Amendment cases, we shall see that the time is ripe for significant overhaul of the regulation of developing technology – and perhaps come to a renewed understanding that, although we do not want to warp the Nation's founding document out of all recognition – to use *only* 18th-century analogies for interpretation does put undue strain on the Constitution, and therefore on the Nation as a whole.

Scalia: A Brief Look

In **Maryland v. King**, respondent King was arrested in 2009 on charges of 1st and 2nd degree assault, both of which carry the possibility of jail sentences. While booking Mr. King in a Maryland county facility, a cheek swab sample of his DNA was taken in accordance with that state's DNA Collection Act. The sample was matched to an unsolved rape from 2003. Although King argued that the Maryland DNA law violated the Fourth Amendment, King was convicted of that earlier crime.

The Maryland court of appeals then found portions of the Act to be unconstitutional. But the Supreme Court held that, when an arrest supported by probable cause is made and the suspect is brought in to be detained, it was reasonable under the Fourth Amendment to take and analyze a cheek-swab DNA sample, similar to taking a photograph and fingerprints.

Justice Scalia dissented in this case; he was joined by Justices Ginsburg, Sotomayor and Kagan. The dissent's argument emphasized the question as to whether or not a DNA sample for "identification" was necessary, given the timing of the sample's entry into the national system *after* the arraignment of the accused. The dissent determined that such identification was not necessary.

In that argument, the dissent might well be correct. The concerns which the dissent raised regarding the privacy of the individual, and the potential for further invasions of that privacy, might well be germane.

Justice Scalia emphasized "identification" via DNA sample in the context of the identifying the accused relevant to the crime for which they are immediately charged. However, "identification" has several meanings, and the reader might wish that Justice Scalia had brought to bear his noted propensity for forensic word definitions. In this case, apparently he did not. The mass-noun definition of "identification" in the Oxford dictionaries is, "The action or process of identifying someone or something or the fact of being identified," with a secondary nuance,: "a means of proving a person's identity …." An additional definition, at the same source, is, "The association or linking of one thing with another." So although Justice Scalia's dissent stresses the identification of Mr. King in and as himself in 2009, it could also be argued that the "identification" was of a previously-unidentified DNA sample from 2003.

The opinion of the Court in *Maryland* v. *King* was delivered by Justice Kennedy, joined by Chief Justice Roberts and Justices Thomas, Breyer and Alito. The Court's opinion emphasized that the collection of a DNA sample was not very invasive – as compared to surgery, for example. The Court further noted that a person under arrest could not expect the same level of privacy as, perhaps, a person on the street; that the time to process a DNA sample continued to become shorter as technical advances continued to evolve; and that Government has interests in the identity of the accused which go well beyond the person's name at the time of the arrest. For example, it is in the government's interest (1) to ensure that the correct person is charged with the crime at issue; (2) to learn if there are factors in the person's past, such as previous extreme violence, which might affect the manner in which law enforcement interacts with the accused, and (3) to discover any potential matches with previously unsolved crimes. It is this last point which came into play in the case of *Maryland v. King*.

The dissent noted a potential for the abuse of such information-gathering. But its analogies strain the logic of the argument, in such examples as traffic stops, TSA (Transportation Security Administration) searches, and the like. On one hand, it is certainly to the protection of "the People" – the Nation's citizens – that restrictions be placed on the collection and use of personal information. On the other hand, without such forms of cross-checking, how is the government to bring to justice the perpetrators of earlier, unsolved crimes? Are we to allow the perpetrator of (for instance) a 2003 rape to "get away with it," simply because the available evidence and technology at the time did not immediately identify a perpetrator?

For the perpetrator to go free at the time but then to cry foul when identified six years later seems an insult to the victim of the crime and to the justice system overall. While some States do have statutes of limitations for rape charges, others do not. Even those states which *do* have limitations may have exceptions, and one of those exceptions involves a later identification via DNA evidence. As it happens, Maryland has no statute of limitations for rape charges.

In **Florida v. Jardines,** police took a drug-sniffing dog to the porch of Jardines's home, where the dog gave a positive indicator for the presence of narcotics. On that basis, police obtained a warrant, found that Jones was growing marijuana in his home, and subsequently arrested him for drug trafficking. The constitutional question was whether or not this search was "unreasonable" under the Fourth Amendment.

Here again, we are presented with "the weight of a feather": there are some reasonable points on both sides of this argument. In 2012, Justice Scalia delivered the opinion of the Supreme Court, in which Justices Thomas, Ginsburg, Sotomayor and Kagan joined. Justice Kagan also delivered a concurring opinion, in which Justices Ginsburg and Sotomayor joined. Justice Alito filed a dissenting opinion, in which Chief Justice Roberts and Justices Kennedy and Breyer joined.

The opinion of the Court, as presented by Justice Scalia, held that the case was straightforward: "use of the trained narcotics dog ... was a Fourth Amendment search unsupported by probable cause" which rendered the resulting information, and warrant, invalid.

But was it invalid?

The investigation was indeed on private property. The

walkway and front porch leading to Jardines's home are part of the area known in legal terms as the "curtilage." (Good crossword puzzle word there.) But the police did not stray – did not troll about in the yard, for example – nor did they spend a great deal of time: perhaps the minute or two that it takes to deliver the mail, or to drop a newspaper on a subscriber's front porch.

Is it distasteful that this investigation took place? Yes. But was it actually illegal?

Justice Scalia noted the State's argument, that an "investigation by a trained narcotics dog ... cannot implicate any legitimate privacy interest" and he compared the case to *Jones*, discussed above. He found that it did not matter whether the government used an electronic device or a trained animal: a data-gathering expedition was just that.

Justice Kagan's concurring opinion raised the issue of privacy as well as that of property. It noted that if a "visitor" comes to the front door with high-powered binoculars to peer through the window, the resident's privacy is unreasonably invaded. And it further noted that a trained narcotics dog has more in common with high-powered binoculars than with the neighbor's pet.

Justice Alito's dissenting opinion noted the license of members of the public to approach a house's front door and to remain there briefly – as took place in this case. This license does not mean that one needs to speak to the occupant. Mail carriers and newspaper deliverers traditionally do not do so. The dissent further noted that a dog is not a new technology or a device, but an effective addition to legitimate law enforcement's tools.

Outcome

New technologies do need regulatory parameters. But they ought not to be forbidden entirely, nor can the ongoing development of "older" technologies, such as a dog, be outlawed. The world will change, whether we will or no, and We the People need responsive lawmaking representatives – to keep up with changing times and to respond on our behalf – not so that we can close and seal a box labeled "future developments" and pretend they do not exist.

For example, we or our representatives need to have thought about the use of drones before the issue comes up – *before* it might be deemed acceptable for a small drone to hover in an alley in order to peer into a bedroom window. Would it matter whether it took place in the daytime or at night? And what would be the "probable cause" for such surveillance – or would it be considered acceptable if the surveillance lead to probable cause for a more invasive search warrant?

Is putting someone to death ever "cruel" or "unusual"?

**The Eighth Amendment:
The death penalty and lethal injection**

***Glossip* v. *Gross* (2015)
Scalia concurred**

The means by which the death penalty is effected, and the prevalence of capital punishment throughout the world, have changed over the past two hundred-plus years. The debate will continue: the case of *Glossip* v. *Gross* (2012) did not solve the Nation's viewpoint on this issue.

Here we see a divided Court. In addition to the opinion of the Court, delivered by Justice Alito and joined by Chief Justice Roberts and Justices Scalia, Kennedy and Thomas, there were two concurring opinions, delivered by Justices Scalia and Thomas, who each also joined the other's opinion. There were also two lengthy dissents: the "principal dissent," delivered by Justice Sotomayor and joined by Justices Ginsburg, Breyer and Kagan, and a second dissent, delivered by Justice Breyer and joined by Justice Ginsburg.

Scalia: A Brief Look

Several of the Justices themselves, in the course of their delivered opinions, pointed out the need for further examination of this issue. It is not really for the Justices to legislate: they can only adjudicate within the law as it stands, and point out the issues for the legislators to examine and revise as the representatives of the People.

The constitutional issue

At issue here is the Eighth Amendment: "Excessive bail shall not be required, nor excessive fines imposed, nor cruel and unusual punishments inflicted."

Summary

As Justice Alito quoted from an earlier case, "Because capital punishment – that is, the death penalty –- is constitutional, there must be a constitutional means of carrying it out." After Oklahoma adopted lethal injection as its method of execution, that State settled on a three-drug protocol: one to induce a state of unconsciousness, the second to paralyze the body, and the third to induce cardiac arrest.

In *Baze* v. *Rees* (2008), the Court held that the three-drug protocol did not violate the Eighth Amendment's prohibition against cruel and unusual punishments. Anti-death-penalty advocates then pressured pharmaceutical companies to prevent sodium thiopental, used as the first drug in the three from being used in executions. When it was later replaced by another barbiturate called pentobarbital, a similar protest followed. When Oklahoma could not obtain either sodium thiopental or pentobarbital, the State began to use a 500 milligram dose of a sedative called midazolam.

Oklahoma death-row inmates filed a claim that the use of midazolam violated the Eighth Amendment: even with a 500-milligram dose, a prisoner would still be able to feel pain during the administration of the second and third drugs. But to succeed on an Eighth Amendment method of execution claim, a prisoner must establish that the method creates a demonstrated risk of severe pain and that the risk is substantial when compared to the known and available alternatives. The lower courts required the prisoners to identify a usable alternative, and they could not do so.

Justice Alito delivered the opinion of the Court. He traced the history of different methods of execution through the history of the Nation, including hanging, the firing squad, lethal gas, and electrocution. As the Nation continued to seek a "more humane" method, late in the 20th century lethal injection was adopted. The opinion noted that the Court has held that the Constitution does not require that all risk of pain be avoided, and that to do so would "effectively outlaw the death penalty altogether." After all, not every death is pain-free, although humans might wish it so. The Court's opinion traced the diminishing availability of the specific drugs selected for this protocol, as lobbyists protested to the specific pharmaceutical manufacturers, both domestically and abroad. Changes in the drugs used in the protocol also highlighted clear discomfort on the part of the condemned during the process of lethal injection, which in turn once more raised the question of the "cruelty" of the particular punishment.

We might turn aside from the Court's opinion for a moment to note that the particular prisoners had inflicted particularly horrific crimes on their victims, and to raise the specter of retribution. Is society leaning towards the retributive justice of "an eye for an eye," or the more pacifistic forgiveness that would seek out "that of God in everyone"?

There are several points wrong, from a moral standpoint, with the opinion of the Court: One, which was pointed out by the principal dissent, is that the prisoners who were bringing action were expected, themselves, to propose an adequate substitute. Underlying that argument is the implication of retributive justice: if the prisoners do not like the means by which they are to die, *they* are expected to propose an alternative? In the field of lethal pharmaceuticals?

Scalia: A Brief Look

Another point was that *none* of these methods are "humane." A firing squad would be more humane. Famously, hemlock tea might be more humane – the poison chosen by the Athenian philosopher Socrates, condemned to death in 399 B.C.E. Even so, none of these methods are free from all pain.

The Court's opinion in the present case noted that "the principal dissent implies that it would be unconstitutional to use a method that 'could be seen as a devolution to a more primitive era.'… If States cannot return to any of the "more primitive" methods used in the past, and if no drug that meets with the principal dissent's approval is available for use in carrying out a death sentence, the logical conclusion is clear." But the Court has affirmed more than once that "capital punishment is not *per se* unconstitutional."

It would not be the first time in this Nation's history that, after much back-and-forth, the Nation changed direction. A glaring example can be found in the National discourse after the *Dred Scott* decision was handed down. Simply because the Court has reaffirmed, time and again, that capital punishment is constitutional, does not mean that it will remain so for all time. (Equally, just because the Church reaffirmed, time and again, that the sun orbited the earth and not vice versa, did not mean that that the assertion was never proven to the contrary.)

In order for this Nation to continue to flourish and prosper, its people, and their representatives, must be prepared to take new ways of thought into account. Humankind did decide that drawing and quartering was inhumane: eventually it may need to consider whether or not *all* capital punishment is inhumane. Justice Breyer's dissent, in cataloging the cruelties of the capital punishment process, may have found that it is equally adequate – if more expensive – simply to lock up the condemned for life.

Justice Scalia's concurring opinion, although sarcastic in its rhetoric ("Welcome to Groundhog Day") pointed out the lack of logic in that the perpetrators of horrific murders might later petition the Court on the grounds that their own deaths might be "cruel and unusual" under the Eighth Amendment. But, he felt, clemency was not the Court's to give. Quoting Justice Thomas's 2008 concurring opinion in *Baze* v. *Rees,* Justice Scalia noted that historically the Eighth Amendment was understood to bar only punishments that *added* pain "to an otherwise permissible capital sentence." But, with the potential unreliability of the lethal injection "cocktail" of drugs, has not this pharmacopeia become a portent of pain? Justice Scalia also noted Justice Breyer's observation that "it is convictions, not punishments, that are unreliable": and that may well be true.

Nowhere in any of the opinions in this case is it evident, but perhaps Congress should enact legislation requiring that *every* potential execution ought to be preceded by DNA testing. Many of those on death row today have been there for many years, and their convictions preceded accurate DNA testing. To ensure that wrongful execution is minimized, further testing for those previous cases might help to ensure that the correct person is in fact punished for a particular crime.

Justice Scalia noted that that capital punishment raised moral dilemmas that have been considered through the ages, and that the Framers themselves disagreed on the matter to the point that they simply passed the question to the People to reconcile. Justice Thomas's concurring opinion emphasized the Constitutional provisions which ensure that capital punishment convictions *are* left to the People, not to "legal elites" in order that the accused may indeed be sentenced by a jury of their peers.

Yet Justice Breyer noted that there were anomalies and inconsistencies: Capital sentencing might only occur in particular geographic areas; it was more likely to occur when the jury and the accused are not of the same demographic; it might be affected if the judge were elected rather than appointed, or if the accused and the victim were not of the same demographic, and so forth.

Scalia: A Brief Look

In his concurrence, Justice Thomas noted the Constitution's Article III guarantee of the right to an impartial jury from the district where the crime took place: but there might still be demographic disparities between accused and jury. Justice Thomas also commented that, if we are uneasy with these "disparate outcomes, it seems ...that the best solution is for the Court to stop making up Eighth Amendment claims in its ceaseless quest to end the death penalty through undemocratic means."

Justice Thomas's concurring opinion and Justice Breyer's dissenting opinion appear to be in agreement on that point. Justice Breyer opened with the statement, "[R]ather than try to patch up the death penalty's legal wounds one at a time, I would ask for full briefing on a more basic question: whether the death penalty violates the Constitution." The death penalty and the Eighth Amendment appear to be broken, and the Supreme Court has been trying to patch up the legal wounds one case at a time.

Both Justices were correct, as was Justice Scalia. It is not for the judiciary, but for the People, to reassess the place of capital punishment in the country's beliefs. The Nation cannot continue to be wholly out of sync with global beliefs and at the same time expect to continue to be the "world's policeman," without doing great damage both to global society and to its own standing in the world. Unless that is the intent of those in power, in which case the first thing to dismantle will be the National Anthem, because the United States of America will *not* be "the land of the free ..." and ought not to pretend that it is.

Justice Breyer's dissent, in which Justice Ginsburg joined, posited three "constitutional defects" involving the death penalty: First, unreliability; second, arbitrary application, and third, delays so long that the death penalty's "penological" purpose is undermined. Justice Breyer detailed the ways in which these had caused the death penalty to evolve into a 'cruel and unusual punishment" under the Eighth Amendment.

Unreliability There are those on death row who have been incarcerated since before the prevalence of DNA evidence, some of whom were convicted in error. Justice Breyer's dissent noted that the finality of death created a "qualitative difference" between the death penalty and other punishments, including life in prison. That difference heightened the need for reliability: once a death sentence is carried out, it cannot be reversed.

Arbitrariness In the 1972 case *Furman v Georgia,* Justice Potter Stewart found the death penalty "unconstitutional as administered." In the present case, Justice Breyer cited numerous studies to indicate that not only is the imposition of the death penalty not always correlated to the heinous nature of a particular crime, but factors that not ought to have an impact on sentencing often do. Such factors might include the race and gender of the victim; the geographical location of the crime – not only by state but by county; the racial makeup of the jury in comparison with the race of the accused; the resources of the county for its public defense program; or political pressures on judges who must stand for election or who sit in smaller communities rather than large cities. All such factors, in sum, add to the arbitrary and inconsistent imposition of the death penalty.

Excessive Delays Almost inevitably, wrote Justice Breyer, unreliability and arbitrariness lead to the problem of excessive delays, where the accused had been condemned but then spent long years on death row. This was not the case when the Constitution was framed: typically, the condemned were executed within weeks or months.

In addition, those long years are typically spent in solitary confinement, for at least 22 out of every 24 hours. An offender sentenced to death has a good chance of dying from natural causes in the intervening years before an execution occurs. The equivalent of a life sentence without parole is a more likely scenario, so that the threat of execution may not act as a deterrent. Lengthy delays undermine the rationale of the penalty of eventual death, while the uncertainty may also heighten the cruelty of the sentence: will it occur or not? Although the delays might have made execution more reliable by allowing time to ensure that those who are innocent or mentally incompetent are not put to death, that element of cruelty was likely not an intent of the Framers of the Constitution.

More "unusual"? The net result is that the death penalty is becoming rarer. Justice Breyer set forth statistics that indicated in sum, that only three States accounted for 80% of executions, and that 66% of the Nation's population lived in States where an execution had not recently been carried out. In sum, at the county level, in 86% of counties in the country, there was essentially not a death penalty. Although he relied in large part on statistics of events (or non-events) in this country rather than internationally, Justice Breyer also noted that "95 of the 193 members of the United Nations have formally abolished the death penalty and an additional 42 have abolished it in practice," and that "the United States was the only country in the Americas to execute an inmate in 2013."

He further noted that the Constitution favors democratic, not judicial, decisions. Those countries which have abolished the death penalty have done so through their legislatures, not their judiciary. (That was the point also made in Justice Thomas's concurring decision.) Justice Breyer concluded that it was "highly likely" that the death penalty violated the Eighth Amendment, and that "at the least" the Supreme Court ought to call for a "full briefing" on the question.

In an impassioned dissent, joined by Justices Ginsburg, Breyer, and Kagan, Justice Sotomayor examined the cruelty inherent in the three-drug protocol used for lethal injections. She traced the history of previous methods of execution eventually determined to be "off-limits," notably the firing squad and the electric chair, and reminded the Court that "there has been little dispute that [the Eighth Amendment] at the very least precludes the imposition of 'barbarous physical punishments'"– which, as this dissent described them, would now include death by lethal injection.

The opinion of the Court, and its concurring Justices, suggested that although it would unconstitutional to *design* a punishment to inflict pain, that would not hold if the pain were inflicted in a sense as a byproduct of the punishment or protocol.

But the primary dissent noted that ends do not justify "any and all means." Barbarity is still barbarity, even if that method of execution is the only one currently available to a State. A State is not required, or forced, to carry out an execution. And it remains the responsibility of the State, not of the condemned, to ensure that the method of punishment is constitutional.

Instead it would seem that requiring the condemned to select a constitutional method of execution is (although dressed up) the equivalent of requiring the condemned to dig their own graves before being shot. We condemn such practices in other nations and regimes: this is no less barbarous.

The interpretation of the Constitution is an ongoing dialogue in the Nation. The ramifications of the Eighth Amendment are certainly ripe for discussion. And, as with so many other events in the Nation at this time – including the refusal of many sports figures to countenance a National Anthem that refers to us, quite falsely, as "the land of the free and the home of the brave" – re-examination of the Eighth Amendment brings us to the basic question: Who are we as a Nation, really? And who do we *claim* to be?

For these are the two sides of the Scales of Justice.

Whether or not one agreed with him, Justice Antonin Scalia's judicial opinions *did* make one think. It is clear that, two hundred and twenty-some years on, we cannot simply roll back the

Scalia: A Brief Look

calendar pages; nor can we determine precisely, in all instances, what the Framers of the Constitution had in mind. We deal with different circumstances than they.

Nevertheless, the Framers designed a governing document superior to, and more resilient than, those governing other nations. Many of Justice Scalia's "originalist" opinions, while impossible to take in whole, do act as one half of the checks-and-balances that keep the governmental ship on course. As the signature duet in the modern opera *Scalia/Ginsburg* expressed it: "We are different, We are one."[2]

---

[2] Wang, D., *Scalia/Ginsburg*, http://lawandarts.org/article/scaliaginsburg-a-gentle-parody-of-operatic-proportions/

The Outcome Overall

It was once said, "Blessed are the flexible; for they shall bend and not break." One of the issues with Justice Scalia's overall thought was that, in trying to preserve the original Constitution, he was at times inflexible. In order for the Constitution to respond to the development of the country – its technologies, its science, and its social issues – it *is* necessary for the Constitution, and for the country's lawmakers, to be capable of some flexibility.

Flexibility is not the same as spinelessness. A tree which is flexible bends in the wind, but it does not lose its essential nature or its shape. It is not flattened: it will retain its strength, snap back to the vertical, and continue to grow. And this is the core of the theory of "living originalism."

Despite Justice Scalia's erudition and his probity, the Nation needs a living Constitution, not a dead one. It needs thoughtful leaders and lawmakers willing to guide the country forward, not to return it to an illusory past which only served a segment of its population.

Respect, civility, thoughtfulness: These are cornerstones of the foundation on which to buttress a lawful nation that can be an inspiration and an example in the world : might and braggadocio are no longer the tenets of right – if ever they truly were. Let us work together to build on the foundations of those 18th-century Framers. Let us understand that the intervening years have brought us the resources and ideas and beliefs of those who have come to this country over time.

America cannot continue to act as if we (or a particular subset of "us") are always right and the rest of the planet is wrong. That way lies destruction – of our standing, our country, our planet.. We have always been a diverse nation, although our fabric has changed as the nation has developed. Let us celebrate that, and our planet, as we share our thoughts, challenges and opportunities with our fellow-nations in the modern world.

Further Reading

Commentary on the Constitution, and on the Justices, is vast and ever-increasing. The interested reader will find many other works available, focused not only to lay readers but also to academic scholars and legal experts.

For the opinions, see www.supremecourt.gov

Amar, Akhil Reed. *The Constitution Today: Timeless Lessons for the Issues of Our Era.* (Basic Books, 2016)

Balkin, Jack M. *Living Originalism* (Belknap, Harvard University Press, 2011)

Biskupic, Joan. *American Original: The Life and Constitution of Supreme Court Justice Antonin Scalia* (Farrar, Straus and Giroux, 2010)

Breyer, Stephen A. *The Court and the World: American Law and the New Global Realities* (Knopf, 2015)

Ginsburg, Ruth Bader. *My Own Words.* (Simon & Schuster, 2016)

Murphy, Bruce Allen. *Scalia: a Court of One.* (Simon & Schuster, 2014)

Power, Robert C., and Mark C. Alexander. *A Short and Happy Guide to the First Amendment.* (West Academic Publishing, 2016)

Rosen, Jeffrey. *The Supreme Court; the Personalities and Rivalries that Defined America.* (Times Books, 2007)

Scalia, Antonin G., and Kevin A. Ring. *Scalia's Court: A Legacy of Landmark Opinions and Dissents.* (Regnery Publishing, 2016)

*The Supreme Court: a C-SPAN Book Featuring the Justices in Their Own Words (*National Cable Satellite Corporation, 2010, 2011)

INDEX

Abuse, potential for,
  in information-gathering, 40, 43
ACLU (American Civil Liberties Union), 13
Aliens, unauthorized, 29, 33, 36-37
Alito, Justice Samuel
  on capital punishment, 48-50
  on intrusion, 41, 45
  on surveillance, 40-41
Amendments to the Constitution, 9, 22, 52. See also *D.C. v. Heller;* Fourth Amendment; *Glossip v. Gross;* *McCreary County v. ACLU*
Arizona v. U.S. (2012), 29-37
  constitutional issue, 30
  Kennedy, Justice, 30, 36-37
  Scalia, Justice, 30-35
Arizona, social services in, 33, 35
Axelrod, David, 8

Blacks. See Ethnicity/race
Blackstone's *Commentaries on the Laws of England* (1760s), 25
Breyer, Justice Stephen
  on death penalty, 51, 52-54
  on established religion, 16
  on firearms control, 26-28

Capital punishment, 47-55
Capital sentencing, consistency of, 51, 53
Civil rights, and state vs. federal power, 23, 24, 25-26, 34-35
Commandments, Ten, display of, 11-18
Congress of the United States,
  immigration and, 31, 36
  review of legislation and, 41, 51
  Supreme Court and, 7-8
Constitution of the United States.
  Marbury v. Madison (1803) and, 25
  Article I, section 8. See *Arizona v. United States.*
  Article II, section 2.
    appointment of Supreme Court justices, 7-8
  Article VI, clause 2.
    Supremacy clause, 30, 37

See also Amendments to the Constitution; Interpretation, Originalism.
Convictions, arbitrary, 51-53
Crime rates, international, and gun laws, 28
Cruel & unusual punishment, 47-55
  lethal injection as, 48, 49, 54
Curtilage, as legal area, 44-45

D.C. v. Heller (2008), 19-28
  constitutional issue, 20
  Breyer, Justice, 26-28
  Scalia, Justice, 21-24, 26
  Stevens, Justice, 24-26
Death penalty
  constitutionality, 48-50, 51, 54
  pain and, 48-49, 50, 54-55
  pharmaceutical firms and, 48-49
Delays, excessive
  capital punishment and, 53-54
Democracy in action, 9-10, 37, 50
  judicial decision making and, 26, 54
Developing technologies,
  "data-gathering" and, 39-45
  regulation of, 45-46
District of Columbia,
  ban on handguns, 20-21, 24
    constitutionality of, 21, 22, 24-27
  federal governance of, 24
  Firearms Control Regulation Act of 1975, 20-21, 26, 27
  local parameters, 21, 26
DNA Collection Act (Maryland), 42
DNA testing
  capital punishment and, 51, 53
  "identification" and, 42-44
Dog, narcotics, 44-45
Drones, probable cause and, 46
Drugs, 48, 49, 54-55

Eighth Amendment, 47-56
  death penalty and, 50-51, 52-55
  method-of-execution claims under, 48-49
  three-drug protocol and, 48
Enslavement. See Human rights issues
Establishment Clause, 11-18
  purpose of display under, 13-14
  Van Orden v. Perry, 15-16
Ethnicity/race
  immigration and, 32
  right to bear arms and, 23, 25-26
Execution(s), 48-49, 50, 53, 55

INDEX

Federal governance of D.C., 24
Federal vs. state law, 29-30, 31-32, 33, 34-35
Federal vs. state power, 24, 25-26, 33, 34-35
Federalist, The, 36
Firearms Control Regulation Act of 1975, 20-21, 26, 27
Firearms, presence of
 death or accident and, 27
Flexibility
 originalist interpretation of Constitution and, 57
Florida v. Jardines (2013), 44-45
 Fourth Amendment and, 38-39, 44
 Alito, Justice, 45
 Kagan, Justice, 45
 Scalia, Justice, 44-45
 use of narcotics dog, 44-45
Foreigners, exclusion of
 sovereignty and, 31
Foundations (of American Law and Government) display, 13, 15-17, 18
Founders (of the Nation)
 as immigrants, 37
 intent, 9, 12, 22
 religion and, 11-12, 13, 14, 17
 weaponry, use of, and, 20, 22
Fourth Amendment, 38-46
 See also Privacy, right to
Framers (of the Constitution)
 capital punishment and, 51, 54
 framework, 9
 gun control policy and, 19, 26
 interpretation of intent, 9, 20, 35, 36, 39, 56
 privacy and, 39
 religion and, 14
 self-defense interest, 24, 26, 28
Funding of Constitutional cases, private, 21

Ginsburg, Justice Ruth Bader, 51
Glossip v. Gross (2015), 10, 47-56
 Eighth Amendment and, 47-48, 51, 52, 55
 Alito, Justice, 48-50, 55
 Breyer Justice, 51, 52-54
 Scalia, Justice, 50-51
 Sotomayor, Justice, 54-55
 Thomas, Justice, 52
GPS device
 U.S. v. Jones and, 39-41
Gun control. See *D.C. v. Heller*
Gun control policy
 Framers of Constitution and, 26
 impact of changing law, 27-28
Gun violence in the U.S.,
 Supreme Court and, 24

Handguns
 ban on
  effect on crime and, 27-28
  ownership in D.C. and, 21, 24, 26
 colonial regulation, 26
 effect of ownership, 23, 27, 28
 presence of, 21, 23, 27
 Second Amendment and, 22
 statistics, 27-28
 utility in 18th century, 28
Heller. See *D.C. v. Heller* (2008)
Heller decision, as example of living interpretation, 26
Human rights issues
 federal v. state responsibility for, 32, 34

Identification using DNA
 individual privacy and, 43
 Maryland v. King and, 42-44
Illegal immigration
 federal enforcement and, 33, 36
 impact of, 29, 34, 35, 36
 Plyer v. Doe and, 33
Immigrants
 competition with citizenry,
  history in America, 32
 ethnicity/race and, 32, 35
 law in history and, 31
Immigration and Naturalization Law, U.S., 31
Immigration policy,
 "destiny of Nation" and, 37
 federal powers, 32, 34-35
 state vs. nation, 31, 32, 35, 36-37
 See also *Arizona v. United States.*
Immigration, illegal. See Illegal immigration
Inconsistencies in capital sentencing, 51, 53
Inflexibility v. flexibility
 Constitutional originalism and, 57
Internationality
 crime rates, 28
 executions, 54
 immigration and, 31, 36
 U.S. constitutional interpretation and, 31, 32-33. 57-58

61

Scalia: A Brief Look

Interpretation, constitutional, 57
  Blackstone and, 25
  Eighth Amendment and, 54
  Fourth Amendment and, 39, 40-41
  Marbury v. Madison and, 25
  originalism and, 9, 19, 22, 40-41, 56
  Second Amendment and, 19-20, 21-22, 23, 24
  Story and, 25
  Supreme Court and, 11, 24-25, 51-52
Intrusion, concept of, 39-40, 41, 42, 43, 44-45. *See also* Privacy, Right to

Judicial lawmaking, 26, 52

Kagan, Justice Elena, 8, 30
  on privacy, 45
Kennedy, Justice Anthony
  on immigration policy, 36-37
  on privacy and identification, 43

Law enforcement
  developing technologies and, 40, 41, 43, 45, 46
  state vs. federal powers, 29-30
Law of Nations (1758), 31
Legislative review
  of capital punishment, 51-54
  of developing technologies, 40, 41, 45-46
Lethal injection, as cruel and unusual punishment, 47, 48-49, 54-55
  See also *Glossip v. Gross*
Living vs. originalist Constitutional interpretation, 9, 19, 22, 40-41, 56, 57

Marbury v. Madison (1803), 25
Marriage. *See* Human rights issues
Maryland v. King (2013), 42-44
  Kennedy, Justice, 43-44
  Scalia, Justice, 42-43
McCreary County v. ACLU (2005),11-18
  secular purpose, 13-17
  O'Connor, Justice, 16-17
  Scalia, Justice, 14-16
  Souter, Justice, 13-14
Method-of-execution claims
  Eighth Amendment and, 48-49, 55
Militia
  definitions, 23
  in Second Amendment, 24-25
Morality, 14-15, 49, 51

Narcotics dog, use of, 44-45
Naturalization. See *Arizona v. U.S.*; Immigration

Naturalization, rule of, 30
Neutrality, religious, 14, 17

New technologies
  DNA identification 42-44
  GPS device, 39-41
  narcotics dog, use of, 44-45
  See also Developing technologies
Noncitizens, treatment/removal of
  outlined by U.S. Congress, 36

O'Connor, Justice Sandra Day
  on religion clauses, 16-17
Oklahoma, and lethal injection, 48
Originalism, 9, 56, 57
  interpretation as, 19, 22, 41
  Second Amendment and, 19, 22, 26
  sovereignty and, 30-31

Pain, 48-51,55
Pharmaceutical companies, 48, 49
Plyer v. Doe (1982), 33
Policies, federal vs. state, 32, 37
Post-Civil War legislation, and right to bear arms, 23, 25-26
Powers, state v. federal,
  civil rights and, 23, 24-25, 33-34
Priorities, state v. federal, 32
Privacy, right to
  changing technologies and,17,41, 45
  curtilage, within, 44-45
  "data-gathering" and, 40, 45
  DNA sampling and, 42, 43
  electronic surveillance
    and intrusions, 40, 41, 45
  in vehicle, in public, 40
  in 21st century, 39, 40, 41
Probable cause
  drones and, 46
  Fourth Amendment and, 39
  Maryland DNA Act and, 42
  narcotics dog and, 44
Providence, Founders and, 13

Race/ethnicity See Ethnicity/race
Regulatory overhaul and changing technologies, 40, 45-46
Religion, neutrality and, 14, 17
Religious effect of Foundations display, 13, 15-17
Religious intent vs. secular purpose, 13-18
Religious wars, Founders and, 14
Resources, allocation of
  county, 53
  federal, and state, 29, 33, 34
Retributive justice, 49

INDEX

Right to bear arms
  ethnicity/race and, 23, 25-26
Right to privacy. *See* Privacy, right to

Scalia, Justice Antonin, 7-10
  and 18th-century analogies, 40-41
  and originalism, 9, 30-31, 56, 57
  Axelrod and, 8
  on capital punishment, 50-51
  on display of Ten Commandments, 14-15,16
  on handgun ownership, 20, 21-24, 26
  on identification, 42-43
  on illegal immigration, 32-35
  on religious tolerance, 14-15
  on searches, 39-40, 44-45
  on sovereignty, 30-32, 33-35
  on translation of the Ten Commandments, 15-16
Scalia/Ginsburg (one-act modern opera), 56
Second Amendment, 19-28
  See also District of Columbia; Handguns; Self-defense.
Secular purpose vs. religious intent, 13-18
Self-defense, right of, 22, 23, 24, 25, 28
Separation of powers,
  church and state See *McCreary*
  state and federal See *Arizona*
Social services, strain on,
  and illegal immigration, 33, 35
Solitary confinement
  and delays in execution, 53-54
Sotomayor, Justice Sonia
  and lethal injection, 54-55
  and surveillance, 40
Souter, Justice David
  on religious display, 13-14
  retirement, 8
Sovereignty
  as constitutional issue, 30
  foreigners and, 31
  international interaction and, 36
  Scalia on, 30-32, 33-35
  state vs. federal, 29, 30, 31, 34-35, 36-37
  unlawful aliens and, 32-33
Statutes of limitations, 44
Stevens, Justice John Paul, 15
  on Second Amendment interpretation, 24-26
Story's *Commentaries on the Constitution of the United States*, 25
Supremacy Clause, 30, 37

Supreme Court, U. S.
  interpretation by, 11, 24
  Justices, appointment of, 7-8
  non-legislative role, 52
  procedures of, 10

Technologies, New or Developing,
  see Developing Technologies; New Technologies
Ten Commandments,
  display of, 11-18
  list of, 12
Thomas, Justice Clarence
  on capital punishment, 51, 52, 54
Three-drug protocol for lethal injection,
  availability for, 48-49
  Oklahoma and 48
Tolerance, religious, 14-15

United States Constitution. *See* Constitution of the United States
United States v. Jones (2012), 39-41
  Fourth Amendment and, 38-39
  Alito, Justice, 40-41
  Scalia, Justice, 39-40
  Sotomayor, Justice, 40
Unreliability
  capital convictions and, 52-53
Unreasonableness,
  searches and, 39-45

Values, universal, 18
Van Orden v. Perry, 15-17. *See also* Establishment Clause; *McCreary County*

Wang, Derrick, 56*n*
Weaponry, 18th vs. 21st century, 22, 28

63

ABOUT THE AUTHOR

Caroline Mather Brown is an independent scholar who lives and works in northern New Jersey.

www.ingramcontent.com/pod-product-compliance
Lightning Source LLC
Chambersburg PA
CBHW061217180526
45170CB00003B/1039